Who Was

Who Was

by

Alex Quel

PUNCHER & WATTMANN

First published in 2022
Published by Puncher and Wattmann
PO Box 279
Waratah NSW 2298

http://www.puncherandwattmann.com

puncherandwattmann@bigpond.com

NATIONAL
LIBRARY
OF AUSTRALIA

A catalogue entry for this book is available from the National Library of

Australia.

ISBN 9781922571335

Cover design by Tim Cronin

Printed by Lightning Source International

This project has been assisted by the Australian Government through the Australia Council, its arts funding and advisory body.

Australian Government

Australia Council
for the Arts

Foreword: Introducing The Poetry
(And Brief Life) Of Alex Quel

Alex Quel was the pseudonym used by David Hu and Alexis Quigley in the various collaborative poems they wrote before Hu's death in 2009.

Collaborative poems come in many forms and answer to many different purposes. There are poets who collaborate to set their life stories, childhoods, personal experiences of class, race and gender alongside the experiences of another, to bring into sharper contrast, both for themselves and for their readers, the different realities faced by people in an unequal divided society. Typically in such a situation each maintains autonomy over her own section, placing her own name above or below her contribution. Others are drawn to collaboration more to see what will happen when surrendering a certain level of control and letting the poem emerge from a combined effort, the poem less as one's story than something other than oneself, possessing an independent beauty or trace of life's varied troubles. A pseudonym, then, might serve to mark that the work no longer belongs to A or B but to something beyond either of them. Play, but purposeful play.

Born in 1972 to a wealthy Chinese-Australian family, David Hu was an architecture student at Sydney University when he first met Alexis Quigley. Several years older than David, Alexis grew up in rural New South Wales, left school early, and then worked at a variety of jobs from barmaid to fashion model, from band manager to fashion consultant, before enrolling herself in a photography course at COFA. It was early in 1993 when they first met.

Restless at the sense of being confined to a single career, a single life trajectory, David took a year's break in his architecture studies, postponed his plan to do a Masters Degree in Denmark, broke off (temporarily) his engagement to childhood sweetheart Amanda Yip, and moved into a shared house in Newtown where, among his three flat-mates, was Alexis. Their friendship blossomed rapidly and soon found expression in collaborative writing, a practice they continued until a few months before David's death from cancer in 2009.

While the first collaborative poems of Hu and Quigley were written between 1993 and 1996, *Who Was* is a work from ten years later. The fun and game-playing of the first collaborations are replaced by a more sombre mood marked by a new sense of life's frailty. David was diagnosed with a rare form of cancer in 2004. By then he was a successful architect, married to Amanda Yip, and enjoying a busy life managing projects in Sydney and Brisbane. But he had always maintained his friendship with Alexis and they had talked at various times about reworking their collaborations into publishable work.

Equally, between their first meeting and their 2005-2008 collaboration Who Was, Alexis Quigley had grown in confidence and acclaim as an artist. She had international success with her photomontage multi-media works *Berlin I am looking at you* and *The Smoking Gun at the End of the Universe*, the latter leading to many spin-offs including inspiring the choreography for a style of flash-mob dancing popular in Southeast Asia. In 2012 she made 'a little splash' (as she put it) with her film, *Poème de l'amour et de la mer*, a feminist remake of Ernest Chausson's classic work for soprano and orchestra set against the background of ecological disaster and imminent nuclear war. It has since gained a cult following and is well-known in circles of 'small group watchers', film buffs who believe appreciation is best cultivated and shared when audience members number no more than fifteen.

The name Alex Quel is both a shortening of Alexis Quigley's two names and a play on David Hu's surname. The butt of teasing at school for his name and looks, Hu experimented with various playful pseudonyms across several languages, such as Kien and Qui and Tell Kell or Quel.

In the spirit of collaboration, given that David Hu is no longer alive to share in the editing process, Alexis Quigley approached MTC Cronin and Peter Boyle to undertake the editing of what was at that stage very much a draft manuscript.

A few more words about the nature of Hu's and Quigley's collaboration in the persona of Alex Quel: In the three years it took to produce the initial manuscript of *Who Was* David found he could, for the most part, with very few exceptions, no longer tell who wrote which lines or sections of poems. In his memory most of this manuscript is Alexis'. In Alexis' memory the poems are very evenly divided between the two of them and she can always tell which lines were written by each of them. It seemed to David, for example, that all of the very short poems were by Alexis, but to Alexis they seem to be as often by David as by herself.

Is *Who Was* an elegy composed collaboratively in the uncertainty of life, including what many experience as the wavering mirage of any stable self, the arbitrary nature of a name and a fate? Like every book of poems it leaves its authors, whoever they may be, to be read by each reader after their own fashion.

Additional Note

The editors decided, with Alexis Quigley's consent, to include as an Appendix a small sample of other poems by Alex Quel. These range from early playful poems, such as "Constellation of the Inebriated" (which she earmarked as Quel's first poem) and "Another Bar", to later, more sombre poems like "The Last Days of Hearing". The final poem in this selection, "Who Will I Be When I am No One", reads like a precursor of *Who Was*, carrying strong overtones of Hu's attempt to make sense of his own mortality. In fact, as Quigley told us, David Hu wrote the first six lines of this poem in 1995 but at that time Alexis had no idea how to complete it. Only after David's death did she add the final lines, constructing what may serve as an epitaph to her late friend.

In the late 1990s Hu and Quigley collaborated on a collection of aphorisms and prose pieces under the title *The Collector of Sand*. At that time they started to see Quel as a collector of sand, a fossicker for all that may seem worthless and expendable but increasingly stands out as what truly defines us. Collaborative poetry as it gathers and recombines lines, images and phrases arising from two very different writers, performing what Eliot aptly described as "raids on the inarticulate", might well be called a collection of sand. For both Quigley and Hu, Alex Quel represented a freedom or perhaps purity of invention that contrasted with the constraints of large-budget populist multi-media work or commercial architecture. As Quel remarks in a fake interview published in *Architects Anonymous*, "It is liberating to go under the radar."

Quel is now – and will no doubt be happy to be – very under the radar. As a last sweep, picking up the 'blips' of poetic energy left by David Hu, and in memory of his inhabitation of Alex Quel, Boyle and Cronin have included at the end of this book two 'notes' written by Quigley and Hu which give a lovely insight into the 'personality' of their artistic collaborative process: a single persona created by two people who met one day because they both needed a room in a house.

Peter Boyle & MTC Cronin

3 October 2017

Who Was

I

The signature on the door
leaves its own first name for sadness.
The stone turned over
stares at all it cannot read.
Here, where the entranceway
is a shadow slipping past, muffled
in afternoon,
coolness refreshes long weariness,
distant summers and your own
private grief at one diminutive
life.

II

There is salvation in processing shit.
And shovelling it.

A mess is a mess even when it was recently alive.

Children left on their own —?
May or may not become inhuman.

Today he imagines everything broken.
Rids the house of the unkempt smell
of unfinished poetry.

Perhaps all his emotions are weak.
Certainly projection is beyond him.

At twenty, the vase on the windowsill
looked out on the harbour
that gazed longingly towards the world.

At thirty-three
the checklist in the waiting room:
STATE THREE REASONS WHY DEATH SHOULD BE POSTPONED
writes:
Making love with my lover
Making love with my lover
Making love with my lover –
then adds
Write great poetry,
Read great poetry.

Ah,
the calculators of fate murmur,
such illusions!

He who might have been
Theophilus or Themistocles
or just
two hands holding the pot of earth
where a flametree burns and grows.

IV

expect

to look

V

There is a halo in his small hand.
The girl threading the hoop notices it
and a bird rising out of the halo
laughs at morning
with all its
pomposity of space.

What if a saint came by at this hour
too early for sunset,
too late for the usual
juggling of weekly accounts.

Or suppose the bicycle mender
was still beside us on the pavement
chatting with pigeons,
straightening the rim
of a journey.

Unaware of any dimension
except time
the man with the briefcase moves on,
his head and back all unprotected
while the halo just above his hand
goes on fading.

Useless and purely singular
it offered us, for one moment,
its everyday light.

VI

Like an apple!
Off-white flesh discreetly peeping
from its red-warrior coat
(green if you're on the other team),
inevitable cores drying
like voodoo dolls
on the front verandah.
When he lines them up they look
like a chess set or aging hourglasses –
sniffing at them or rearranging does nothing
to reduce their inscrutability.
Apple smell, he thinks, is a monument
to smells.
The fizzy bead of juice
reminds him he has lips.

Wind across leaves.

Woven texture of octagonal vestments

exonerated by the sun.

Lives inspected by the growth of grass.

VIII

at the edge

of a vessel

was this

IX

The weary book had held him too long.
He looked up where the air was falling
in bright chunks,
where the grit of yesterdays
spun heedless.
All there was
was seeing.

The hour when life wakes you up in your coffin.

X

as if never

without doubt

always as if

XI

At the hour when everything finally stops –
on the great ring-road nothing moves.
A language of lights probes stillness.

XII

An audience of ten thousand.
Mirrors, trees, buses, cars, overhead
        bridges, bleak decay and birds
cheerfully ignoring us while eyes
closed in the steam of their tea, people
still asleep in houses
        or dreaming in windows
shuffle the necessary papers.

In the front seat the driver forgets his name
and the name for the roadway, the side-
        street, the approaching suburb, all
the suburbs crammed with childhood and
        the old, stuck, dying, in
the web of their lives.

He listens: Machine sounds
and at whatever is the greatest distance from here,
soundlessly soft
                branching shadows painted
on the surface of water scoffing
        at a line of reeds turning
their heads only when
                the wind orders.

It begins in the next room.
She is ironing the sky:
folded ripples of blue
float through the trembling window.
Left behind in a mirror
my face is the open morning.
He is already the only name
I recognise.
Did I come here just to recite
all the truths no one needs?

XIV

WHO WAS

XV

Whose dress is hanging on the world?

It seems always as if he is standing on the pardon mat,
kneeling somewhere in a woman's chest
as he tries to make her naked.
But when she's delicious, he's so sky.
Sorry to be able to.
Cost. Most.
Every second he recants his eyelids, her gasps.
Even his laughter seems to suffer
because that's what happens when you have a day.

XVI

tomorrow opening

                                          its door

which you can never enter

                                          from today

The river divides him from himself.
He accepts that no book will mediate
what the dust says to the dust.

'Ten scars.'
Double what you said.

Whatever the dust says to the dust
is missing from those
engaged with sedition and public order.

The river divides us from ourselves.
The book separates us from our words.

XVIII

windworded

                              outgivings

XIX

A stream runs away from itself.
Alone it understands
our hunger to vanish and endure.

A stream passes over itself.
We rise and fall
with the same chaotic atoms.

Enduring to vanish,
vanishing to endure,
everything finds its level.

XX

On the underground stairs
　　　　the lights are gone.
Lit up by all the distance you have come
　　　　your way twists into a luminous
　　　　departure.
Not much survives:
　　　　names peeled off tickets,
　　　　a freak wind along the platform.

You imagine the sky outside –
　　　　all the trains arriving in some
　　　　subterranean Venice.
One slurried speck of grey along the skin,
　　　　the gist of things
　　　　chanted over, some song
　　　　in the wrong language.

In windows high up
　　　　across canals of green paint
　　　　the sun in one salute remembers you.

XXI

Or else this is some life you have never known

and whatever it is can be a million things.

What looks like a city might be

that poor old cow's rump

the day you left.

There, approaching you, notebook in hand,

the silkworm from a forty-year-old shoebox.

Childhood friends waving their forgotten hands,

smiling from forgotten faces.

All your actions remember you.

Your climbing still in the tree.

Around the side of the tin shed, still hiding.

High up, the tree is the colour.

Night returning again and again

to your house.

Is that darkness brought uninvited with the light?

XXII

The Papacy of dim remembrance

and two starlings

have divided the world between them

by secret protocol.

The simplest creatures carry their own space

with them, assert

the order of the immediate.

The temptation to seek our hidden name

in stretched-out time

haunts us. How many

dead orders we create to encase us,

self-hijacked and nailed

to the remade sky.

or a tree

leafless

XXIV

you also IMAGINED

XXV

The astronomers, each with different-
sized telescopes are all simultaneously
gazing at the same star at varying
moments of its evolution.

Demarcations are between their theories
but do not exist
between the star and its selves.

What do the heavens not tell us
because their power of expression
is otherwise occupied?

All of all was gasped once,
is still being gasped —

We fail to grasp it,
brains wagging beyond the lens.

The quick stealing.

A breath.

He looks up déjà vu

because he feels like he's done it before.

He tries extending the length of the air in.

Doing it shorter.

When he feels like he might faint

he stops.

Tries to forget he's doing it.

Realizes his blood is not an image.

Feels no more despair

for what feels like might be seconds

stretching to some other end

of time.

With his dilapidated Spanish
he takes up residence on the ceiling of an ant-palace.
    The ants mumble over him
from a place he already forgets.
    It is the nowhere he starts from
and the word follows him everywhere,
doorway to a quite specific place,
brass-plate on the imagined wall

growing wherever happiness threatened.

XXVIII

Is that the walls of the pot ringing?
Fired by his immanent death.
In him with such delicacy.
Such modesty.
Chairs whose thoughtful legs
do not touch the ground.
Words which cause no destruction.
Which fall to the children and go no further
towards destruction.
Yesterday and tomorrow both
in the breast presented.

For what?

There can be no waiting for all that's done.

What was written impairs itself.

Declares against the everlasting.

The adorning point was reached and passed.

What was fifty years away today

and five hours tomorrow

is behind the shut gate.

He stands in this place where he cannot see

and the skin prickles around his eyes.

Around his head, which appears to them

as a bright spot, swirl the leaves

of the great poets.

On history he can finally turn his back, sand-filled

and not so harsh a place really

for having lost him it invites no prayer of recovery but sits

as if poured into silence.

XXX

He walks by the sea he remembers.

And the wall falls in love with the wind.

With the rain and sun, slab by chunk by rock by grain
by the walking leg of a crustacean.

Unencumbered, empty of history, he waits
for it to pass over the surface of the water.

When he was alive
he had a kind of intimation of what it would be like
when the animals were gone.

He remembers his first death.

Told by the ocean in roundelay.

Sand flung!
Of the billion billion, this speck is just born.

XXXI

despite dusk

despite dawn

dreadfulness

of the moth's wings
shielding the bending flame

folding men
to their chests as if mistakes

— —   —

there is lit a door
whose threshold is broken

                                        only

by the present

this truthless now
fluttering

                                    in all of us

XXXII

This is what happens on both sides of the tree —

The bird doesn't search
for the sky.

Making love with difficulty

effortlessly
your lover's breath merged into yours.

XXXIII

More ever.
How much blackness can exist
in a circle the size of blindness?
And is that its shape
or simply the shape it desires
above all others, shanghais
and drags
to the trump of a skull?

XXXIV

Under the lake of skyward umbrellas
you release the life-full pain
you did not know you had.
Black rings, eyes to the leaden universe
exhale.

He wades into the topography of night.
The stars plot the course of his vanishing:
man who mistook the scattered chaotic suns
for an alphabet.

XXXV

Sometimes existence is a threat.

To an acceptance of death.

To gently, gently, removing want.

He sits killing his thoughts as they arise.

Comparison is the murderer.

Worth is worthless.

XXXVI

Why did he wake and worry about the facts?
As the darkness faded he would wonder
do we all sleep on islands that fear discovery.
Middle worlds floating ideally without touching
the fascinations of happiness, of pain.
With dread he would reason idly on, with every
convolution moving further away from his dreams
which were less fictitious than his thoughts.
Random phrases breaking loose
from the day's rising silt –
'I suggested to her'   'It strikes me'   'Equally'
Does he have a totally unnecessary vocabulary?
What shall he do when the morning appears
like a link to his next shiver, to his next unproved
moment, actions that will become crucial
if he is to explore the matter of his life any further?
He supposes then that the sun is spontaneous
enough and he, himself, the recidivist.
The redemption is in how his foot moves over
the bedside until it reaches the floor.
He will be nothing better or worse in his approach
to first get relief and then to deal with restlessness,
the secret of loneliness he is compelled, like us all,
to share with everyone.

XXXVII

'Not yet.'

He is stopped by a finger to his lips.
Steadied before he speaks.

XXXVIII

Sometimes a person is born with a name
so beautiful you cannot
simply let it rest there;
this name must be grown
steadily on a diet
of wild stars,
it must be shared
between neighbouring galaxies
and made available
for the collective adventuring of squirrels
in search of other landscapes –

a name to orient a cosmos
like the silver dazzle of the poplars
trekking off at dawn
beyond the terrifying mountain.

XXXIX

Here at the end of summer and winter
the light is so absolute
it is enough.

On the island of all his days
three languages jumbled,
three languages tossed by the luminous juggler
who wills the summer as his witness.

One steadied him
with its list of all known banalities.
One terrified with its sonorous boom.
One returned the openness of his gaze,
hand to its lips, signing 'Not yet'.

Three languages
fabricating their own version of the island.

One set up clocks,
TV sets wired to define normality,
limitless shopping malls that mirrored the sea.

One constructed its temples, its
deities of surrender, its banner of collective
departure.

One kept extending itself to capture the sky's curve,
the vanishing flight of birds,
to be the inventor alone in his inventions.

Winds intersect the island.
The palm trees shiver in all they know of night.
Three languages stumbling
into a purely private abandonment.

One offered instructions
on the making of omelettes.
One proclaimed in precisely measured tones
a speech that had lost its content.
One continued to pirouette
in the difficult space of love and death.
With no hands, no props, no bribes,
it dwelt in its own silence.

XLI

On the road that was
you step into the nothing
because it was there.
Just so his foot is drawn
into the black spot, an ink drop
on an infinite pavement.

XLII

A kitten died
at the centre of both your hands.
Grief sat around by a pool filled with leaves.
Sparks of the great burning
wandered the sky at random.

SPARKS

                        sparks

                    (the conversation
always burns itself back to its edges –

a frog choking on its chain at the far end of the universe,
a valley of snails nibbling its way towards the sky –)

Your hand is the desert where the spark goes out.
Nothing is warmer than your palm
when you take it away from my flesh.

'Everything leaves.'
'Nothing escapes.'

How did you stay under the sea, alight?

White and frilled banners of a country called sadness
perpetually forgetting the body you housed.
Wind-blown ever-chattering freshness
that carries no word for yesterday.

Dapper chill regiment of belongings.
Shadows lit by greenery.
Inexplicable symphony borrowed from the universe:
this will outlive us —

XLV

Rain falls
in small uneven drops
and leaves have almost blocked the narrow stream.
In some intimate dialect
sealed from all translation
I can hear the early morning
poetry of the world.

What do you see
when you sleep gazing into blindness?
Though you are round and silent
there is a pinprick of pain you lean towards.
The steady thud of blood
builds up over your world –
no one knows
this living with annihilation.

XLVI

Is this your memory?

Where the reeds fall the bird fell –
All day aiming towards death –
taking the words out to grow them in the sky,
your gutfull life, the unpacked words
and the music weeping inside itself
threading a tune of tomorrows
from sheer habit.

XLVII

I make your face of leaves,

footsteps, turned-away eyes.

I make it with the distant thunder of a clear day

and the smooth water from a hidden cave,

the entrances collapsed,

jagged, light-

denying.

Once I believed this
was something I reached through the sky
to get.
It had the purity of a bird
no longer restricted
to flight.
Do you think I have the image of you
burned to the wall
of my mind
like a shadow caught by a bomb's
spectral heat?
Physics does not seduce me.
Nor this fear.

Your hands?

.

L

They contained a trace
of the feather's oil, the reedy-
stink of the pond but an hour
past, perhaps dirty grass and the smells most
found in rain.
Sweat in your hair
at the side of your face.
I smelled you and I touched you.
I said 'I want a man to help me
as if I was a blind woman.'

A scientist is forbidden to put

his hands on me.

You are not a scientist.

A philosopher cannot touch me.

You are not a philosopher.

I don't even want to lie down

with a poet but I think you understand

how you are not a poet.

You can't be one with my body.

Your hands?

You are asking me about your hands.

They keep changing into the hands

of the man you are capable

of being.

Found on the mudflats where
the river has curved into the sky
these rounded stones that carry names:

"collector of raindrops",
"jade echo", "the heart is a small house"

so birds cry
along the broken river.

Do you still have the book
you couldn't drown?
All the worlds flow through it —
mountains, rivers, cities,
winters and summers.
It clouds with fruitfulness and rage.
It knows about the beautiful body
that once accompanied it
but holds back from all
meddling with fate.
Water is a favourite element
but fire also excites it —
all the crackling, all that
transformation to glowing ash
of something that will not burn.

That book taught you
that love is not an emotion,
that dying is refusing to choose.
All your choices are reading it.
It is written in depth.

LIV

You sealed up your residence in the sky.
Even though the earth still had charms.
There were days for those things.
Only when a hand came tapping for you,
only then was it clear
how far you had come.
In advance of the world
at the boat's prow
a small light shining:
skiff on a lake guided by minimal tremors,
the helmsman without hands,
boat that knows where the world goes.

LV

The signature on the door leaves the name
of the opposite of loneliness –
independence.

The stone creates a world
and in it the stream sings.

Appendix

Further Poetry & Writing by Alex Quel

Constellation of The Inebriated

(The Friend And His Friend
Enter Through The Door Of The Bar)

The lizard, the dolphin and the swamp dump
their romantic elbows at the door to the bar.
The scotch and tea are to be taken with cake
as new names assigned to the crow and liar,
the pale, the great, the herdsman so sincere,
dogs looking for dogs, virgins for four-legged
winged-things, little male dipper for the bear.
It is here where the stars line up in meaning-
less meaning that the cells of the mind align
themselves according to the nose's numb tip,
the softer sponge behind the forehead's sign.
Everything here points to the greatest crew,
the constellation of the haunch, catastrophes
of tonne and wood and fire, what rests hewn
from desire, incomplete arrows in the trees'
half-flesh, pain like swans the wind's blown
this way on its path to another well-lit galaxy.
So go weaving, stumbling but never losing
the tankard's skewered tilt, fine little dipper
lurching precarious as might pernod clouding
a thunderburst or a tenth tequila tranquilizing
a toucan, only shelter under this serenely silent
constellation where wind hammers the striped

pyjamas of painlessness. Navigating by this
may be to stand in the pure chemistry of hot
devastation. Holding nothing. Almost-poet.

Date unknown, early 1993

Another Bar

THIS WAS REPORTED IN THE REPORT
BY THOSE WHO LOGGED THE LOG:

They were each drunk on the cosmos
that belonged to the other.

'I am what God understands'
wrote he.

'What God understands I am'
wrote she.

Clearly, one swig after another
although the sober world

might misapprehend that
the mutual two never met,

that they did not share a farmhouse
or sit together on the pier at the edge

of a country that would come into
being after a revolution of souls.

'Because there are no revolutions'

said he.

'Because we revolted against them all'
said she.

'Sober Postscript to the Report' – to be read only when
drunk

Midnight on the moon
made the solitary barstools set off for other lands.

The Phantom Girl of Belo Horizonte began to see
the space at the end of the corridor where memories can't
go.

And because France
is a suburb in Spain

and Spain is a small lake in South America
with a long Portuguese shore,
any Parisian cyclist
might meet the long-found Luisa Porto.

The grub that devoured
the plantation owner's budding lemon tree

is the butterfly that lands
on the drowned woodcarver's heart.

The rain that falls through the narrow window of the soul
speaks a clear, always-open language.

Because there is sadness
and because there is joy (and immense laughter)

the balloon was stuck in the tree
leaving a slight burn mark on each one's disbelieving hand

so that he settled down to the sun in Rio
while she stayed on in the all-night dancing bar in Solesmes.

December 1993

His Whole Life

He walked around the middle
of a night
three years before I was born.

I wanted to tell him
I was the next lover
but that history had chosen us as an experiment.

He would say everything
I wanted to hear
while I lay in the bed

of the universe with only
the rain and mist and snow to listen
to his words.

He thought I was silence.
And this simply because
he could not teach me to speak.

I still cannot.
Each time I try to reply his whole life
steps between us.

No words pass beyond the imminent death

that deafens his desire. I say Love me.
Then wordless he does.

June 1994

Grief

For ten days he lives outside life
camping on a hillside where the goats nuzzle his tent.
His body becomes a temple to death,
it no longer acknowledges stars.
Cheerful weeds grow from his eyes and scrotum.
He paces himself to the spiders
in their attempt to insert a thread of language
between the wind and the wind.

Waking at midday on the twelfth day,
to the ghost who labours uphill
to lug a pitcher of water for his stink,
for the dry sand of his breath,
he utters a curt "Thanks"
as if the living might expect that much of comfort,
as if the dead after all couldn't help themselves
feeding the seed that speaks,

summoned to give what it takes
even when it takes everything.

January – March 1999

Maturity

it starts with a toothache

the bones are born first in this simple grave
'choose your mask behind your mask'

A world sparks off from the shrug of a shoulder
from the splicings that reveal
we cannot choose

my name in you
can be identified
your internment occurs
naturally in mine

in the drained limelight that is simply
the sentry man's surveillance post
my eyes stare into the nudity
of two suddenly aged feet
bare on a whitewashed floor

the bones know the measurements of their birthplace
gone to ground yearnings
leach into the over-ripe air

maturity is always being sorry

12 September 2002

The Last Days of Hearing

Being without you hearing me.
With my arm around your neck, fifty years pass.
Outside this conversation there are no other sounds.

A pear a fruit a peel
a core shredded to a paste of soundlessness
the black pip the silence bone
centring the hand ...

Sound of you.
Of you loving.
Wind in the leaves saying.
As a tree moves by dropping its seeds.
By dropping its seeds.
The hand.
Dropping its seeds.
Your hand.
Centred on me.
I hear your hand on me.
Making so many adjustments.
Is the sound a gift or a burden?
Loving.
As if you could bear the silence.

There the chestnut trees unfolding

and there the elm writhing to where
the wind gathers its certainty of light
and there
the mango the papaya tree
shrouded in a grey mist of whirring

and across waters your hand reaching finding ...

The single moon.
In a blue sky, no cloud
the moon alone
listening for the fall of the chestnuts
thudding like your heart
against the muffling ground.
Only a moon, porous
addressing the papaya –
She is young.
Take her from her country
to the trees.
Tell her whatever you need to.

October 2005

Who Will I Be When I Am No One

I awake without history,
touching strange hands.
There are mirrors in long corridors
that no longer give back names.

Like a portrait
in which the background so dominates
only a faint cry is there
where a fleck of whiteness was,

I am the room without me.

begun by David Hu in 1995
completed by Alexis Quigley, February 2010

The Collector of Sand (excerpt)

Don't collect anything but sand. All other collections will make
unreality. None of it is real. The collectors of those collections are
not real. If one of them lives in a city, that city ceases to exist. If
they have 204 bones in their body, those bones dissolve. They lose
their socks. They lose their homes. They lose their culling ability.
They can't speak, spell or clear arguments. At first they might
sink their chins to their chests – as if in resignation – but this
does nothing to save their heads or their resignedness. They do
no more scratching and no more holding out. To collect anything
but sand is to invite and realize what cannot constitute absence.
On the other hand, all the little sand grains you can muster have
a pleasant substance. They allow both building up and breaking
down whilst losing nothing. Not even the nothing of nothingness.
That this has been proven over and over again may not prevent
you from gathering together a china cabinet's worth of miniature
ceramic owls. But their disproof isn't worth a hoot.

All collections, bar that of sand, invite the question why.

The Collector keeps his sand in sand's place. Everything helps
to carry it there – ants, the wind, the broom, the soles of his feet
and the treads of his shoes. Sand is the only thing that when
collected is where it is meant to be. Even displaced it is newly
home.

Sandcastles? Hourglasses? What slips through your fingers? How many grains of sand added up to these questions?

Have you heard of being sand-blind? It means to be half-blind. But what is affected by sand – the blindness or the seeing? What does it mean to not see half?

If you would speak to water and expect what you say to be of any consequence, you must be able to read the following two sentences differently: Nothing manifests without you.
                                                      Nothing manifests without you.

It profits one to remain undrowned.

What numbs and blunts if one seriously tries to complete it, may free or open up if approached as play or erasable practice. (De)fining oneself: about ending, limiting, finishing, putting the last, ineradicably exact, nail in the coffin of something that lives and evolves. Here the boundary stone, here the brick wall. But, as play, to define yourself or work on defining oneself may be to invent and then recite the irrepressible synonyms for the one accurate monosyllable "This".

As for destruction, sand always travels both ways. Towards and away from building.

Waves and breath make the same sound – one slowly shapes the planet's body, the other its mind. Complimentary magic, if you mix them you drown.

Alex Quel
7 July 2003

Aphorisms from *The Collector of Sand*

The collector of sand wades out, case in hand, then wakes as a severed hand eaten by ants.

The sharp keening of the trees speaks with a new insistence the day we first gaze into the wounded wild animal of ourself.

Heavy feather of night. Moon crouched in bloom. Moth wind. Through trees, trees and river's ardour rests on a cloud.

Under the waves there are no more magic stones.

A mountain slips in quietly, inventing winds. It was close to the sun – shadows' breach, holding itself up with god's vertebrae.

The cold wind welcomes its lover. It takes so long to see what you've destroyed.

Casting my net towards the stars, all the small rages fill me like a tiny bottle.

What the collector of sand harvests is an immense sandscape undulating to a syntax of generosity.

In this very instant the day holding back one thousand shadows, behind each shadow a sun.

Alex Quel
January 2004 - December 2005

Letter to be Placed in a Bottle

(Memos from the Sand Collector)

Telescopes, ants and old mountains all live by the laws of perspectives, but for each it is their own law. One can give very specific names for creatures and things but does the corvus crassirostris know itself by any name? How much does it help to be five rungs further along the scale of specification when staring at extinction? A world in madness claws towards.

~•~

He has written his name in the corner. His signature resembles an insect spinning on its back. He puts it in his mouth – like a child he must still store everything there. His name and his shadow. It struggles into a word to escape his lips. (A simple breath won't do.) In the air around his face it grows until he is freighted outside himself with how he is known. "You said that is who you are" they said. Anything is bound to happen he thinks, including these things he has been forced to write.

~•~

I bury the box of unread books. There is a dog in my neighbourhood with a nose for good conversation. He comes sniffing around when the gardener says "The cemetery was here from the beginning."

~•~

The testimony is in our hands — the lines are angular, too sharp and there is too much space between words. For now they could be confessionals: "I was having an affair — so that is what it was" but the paper, the large script, the squarish alien look tells us otherwise.

Isolated in what was or how they fell they were there, up there, and the strangeness is what remains.

~•~

It is so small, what we have. We know so little of it and already we have to start using past tenses. Sainthood in the city. The past gathers and scatters us, the trees gather and scatter us. We can barely look the world in the face. And yet we are the world. Other things equally carry their otherness, imperfectly breathe it out, then die. Imagine the cycle formed by a tree crashing into the earth, dissolving slowly downward and outward, then, later, simultaneously, over millennia, rising altered and elsewhere, electric secretions and pheromones leaking out to the edges of the stars. Who is it who was?

Alex Quel
12 -22 September 2005

Notes

In Memory of David Hu

June 6 1995: Tasks for today

* bicycle into town - check for missing package at Post Office and withdraw more cash
* buy asparagus, butter and eggs for tonight's omelette (remember: my turn to cook - Amanda on extra shift, plan for 8:30)
* complete roofing design for apartment complex
* contact Alexis {snail mail?} : query - can any of these poems be completed? if not why not?
separate (or additional) puzzle:
why confident when writing poetry collaboratively, not at all individually? Does this have to do with the way architects work? think? ditto for Alexis with her rock band (her life?)?
* map out some ideas on what could go with Alexis' phrase 'the collector of sand'? Is this character male, female?

possible lines to send to Alexis:

what the face feels
liberated from the torso

one day to be that smooth rockface
the storm winds scream across

a voice saying "back"   "now further back"
stage directions from the other side of space

David Hu, 1995 diary long-version

white fish
cherry tomatoes
cucumber
bunch coriander
cat litter
glass cleaner spray or refill
large stickytape
walnuts
cous cous
CHECK RICE

david lunch on sat amanda?
(or night)

fate squeezed tight as the knot of death (which never
unravels????) – maybe not right now / immense end that avoids
me / there (these?) are our ruins

                                              ???

e.m forster: 'all over. wish I had never written tell no one.'
or something

are the things you see inside your eyes reflected in a mirror?
stupid!

living is so clandestine   **ring denise re pantry door
dying is so clandestine

SEND STUFF OUT, do you want me to do it, prefer oz or os first/
both

~~check re introducing a new collector~~

out on the streets with cash in their sentences

I have my own words, you know, for death...

new short bio for a.q; <u>don't forget</u>

tell him about ernst meister!!

Alexis Quigley, 2009
last jottings for collaboration (written on shopping list)

Who Was

Query – can any of these poems be completed? if not why not?
[p.90]

This is a book about death and failure; about the impossibility of writing about mourning. Mortality and annihilation lie at the heart of these dense and concise traces between empty margins. It is such absence and loss that allows language to speak. At the heart of the strategy that makes this possible is the use of the heteronym.

In his letters Keats speaks of a 'disquisition' he had with Charles Dilke during a walk back to Hampstead from a Christmas pantomime in London. It was as a result of this talk that, as Keats said, 'several things dovetailed in my mind'. For Keats, Dilke was a man who always wanted to know where he stood, 'who cannot feel he has a personal identity unless he has made up his Mind about every thing'. Thus he 'will never come at a truth as long as he lives; because he is always trying at it'.[1] It was Keats' reaction against the continual searching after fact and reason typified by Dilke that decided him as to:

> what quality went to form a Man of Achievement especially in Literature & which Shakespeare possessed so enormously – I mean Negative Capability, that is when man is capable of being in uncertainties, Mysteries, doubts, without any irritable reaching after fact & reason.[2]

> as if never
> without doubt
> always as if [*Who Was* p.21]

What he also called 'diligent Indolence'.[3] Shakespeare's ego dissolves into the world about him, permitting the world to take over. It is, therefore, universal. Milton's ego, on the other hand, is always present and has a tendency to impress itself upon the world. Shakespeare's world creates his art; Milton's art creates his world.[3] Milton's is passion modified by contemplation. He 'takes the imaginative part of passion – that which remains after the event, which the mind reposes on when all is over, which looks upon circumstances from the remotest elevation of thought and fancy and abstracts them from the world of action to that of contemplation'.[4] It is epic rather than dramatic. Milton had a reason for writing, and with this objective he organised the world artistically to fit his purposes. 'He thought of nobler forms and nobler things than those he found around him. He lived apart in the solitude of the own thoughts carefully excluding from his mind whatever might distract its purposes or alloy its purity, or damp its zeal'.[4] Dilke comes under the heading of the Miltonic, whose personal identity depended on his search for a truth and on satisfying himself as to what it was. On the other hand, the 'poetical Character', the character 'which Shakespeare possessed so enormously', has no identity of its own, least of all some special kind of identity which can be called 'poetic'. 'A Poet is the most unpoetical of any thing in existence; because he has no Identity'. He willingly grants that identity to an other leaving 'the poem less as one's story than something other than oneself, possessing an independent beauty or trace of life's varied troubles'. [*Who Was* p.5]

Or:

> the helmsman without hands,
> boat that knows where the world goes
> [*Who Was* p.65]

The boat, not the helmsman. Another way of saying the same thing is to say that it is not the poet but language that speaks (*Die Sprache spricht*). This is Heidegger's formulation which he first formulated in his 1950 lecture 'Language' and frequently repeated it in later works. Adorno wrote that language 'acquires a voice' and 'speaks itself'.[5] Journalese or everyday language is like a tool that we use to convey meaning from one mind to another as accurately as possible. It is a tool used to make concepts more easily understood. It is Miltonic. Like a tool, poetic language, only draws attention to itself when it fails, only speaks when it denies itself as such, when it withdraws and asks us to attend to it with care, to allow the silence at the heart of the withdrawal of the word to speak.

Poetry is not written but writes itself, it is not an effort that invents poetic applications for philosophical points of view. It requires the poet not only go to the edge but also go to the edge of language, to that liminal space that holds together the silence at the ground of the spoken word and the coming into language of the word. In this light Keats wrote to Bailey that the poet awakes and finds the reveries of the imagination to be truth,' whether it existed before or not' and hence 'what the imagination seizes as beauty must be truth'.[6]

Assertive thinking is the reverse of poetic thinking. One assaults language, while the other renounces it. One demands that language reveal, the other accepts that what language reveals of itself is a shyness of revelation – a love of withdrawal, the denial that we all sense at the heart of great poetry. Demands are made of one that serves and assertive thought takes language as servant. Renunciation accepts the reverse – that it is we who serve language and that its revelation lies within its gift. 'It is the nowhere he starts from / and the word follows him everywhere' [*Who Was* p.38]

In some intimate dialect
sealed from all translation
I can hear the early morning
poetry of the world. [*Who Was* p.57]

For Keats, a poet is 'camelion', 'he is continually in for – and filling
some other Body'. So, whereas 'Men and Women who are creatures
of impulse are poetical and have about them some unchangeable
attribute, the poet has none, no identity'.[7] In the third of his
lectures on the English poets, Hazlitt wrote of Shakespeare that
he: 'was the least of an egotist that it was possible to be. He was
nothing in himself; but he was all that others were, or that they
could become'.[8]

One offered instructions
on the making of omelettes.
One proclaimed in precisely measured tones
a speech that had lost its content.
One continued to pirouette
in the difficult space of love and death.
With no hands, no props, no bribes,
it dwelt in its own silence. [*Who Was* p.52]

or again:

three languages jumbled,
three languages tossed by the luminous juggler
who wills the summer as his witness.
One steadied him
with its list of all known banalities.
One terrified with its sonorous boom.
One returned the openness of his gaze,
hand to its lips, signing "Not yet".
[*Who Was* p.51]

and that 'not yet'

> 'Not yet.'
> He is stopped by a finger to his lips.
> Steadied before he speaks. [*Who Was* p.48]

Of Shakespeare Borges writes:

> He had become instinctively adept at pretending to
> be somebody, so that no one would suspect he was in
> fact nobody. In London he discovered the profession
> for which he was destined, that of the actor who
> stands on a stage and pretends to be someone else in
> front of a group of people who pretend to take him
> for that other person.[9]

The poet withdraws asking 'who will I be when I am no-one?'
[*Who Was* p.81] It is not the poet who speaks, who has no voice
who transfers a thought in his mind via words to create a thought
in the reader's mind. Rather, it is language that speaks. The
poet remains, ideally, absent. The poet is always heteronymous,
withdrawing in place of the word. Keats writes that, 'nothing
startles me beyond the moment' and continues, 'If a Sparrow
come before my Window I take part in its existence and pick
about the Gravel'

> the helmsman without hands,
> boat that knows where the world goes
> [*Who Was* p.66]

The ideal poet is non-existent, is taken over by the poem which
displaces her. Indeed, both have withdrawn into death 'from
whose bourne no traveller returns' as 'David could no longer
always tell which lines were written by each of them'. 'The name

Alex Quel is both a shortening of Alexis Quigley's two names and a play on David Hu's surname'[Intro]. Of course, Hu and Quigley become Quel — or Kien or Qui (who exactly? Hu?) Of course, Hu and Quigley brcome Quel — or Kien or Qui (who exactly? Hu?) But these poets may well themselves be heteronyms for others. This is a multi-dimensional game of withdrawal which Pessoa would have loved.

And thus, the heteronyms, the poet written by the other avoids the act of writing, of saying and allows the other into the poetic. The poet no longer knows what she has written or how it came to be. There is always the question.[9]

> 'unfinished poetry' was 'a mess when it was recently alive [...] There is salvation in processing shit' [*Who Was* p.12]

The secret is in the 'might have been' [*Who Was* p.13]

Keats' urn is silent and it is the silent urn that:

> canst thus express
> [...] more sweetly than our rhyme

> it dwelt in its own silence. [*Who Was* p.52]

Or again:

> On history he can finally turn his back, sand-filled
> and not so harsh a place really
> for having lost him it invites no prayer of
> recovery but sits [*Who Was p.40*]

and, for Quel here is the difference between Dilke and Keats:

> One offered instructions
> on the making of omelettes.
> One proclaimed in precisely measured tones a
> speech that had lost its content.
> One continued to pirouette
> in the difficult space of love and death.
> With no hands, no props, no bribes,
> it dwelt in its own silence. [*Who Was* p.52]

or again:

> Why did he wake and worry about the facts?
> As the darkness faded he would wonder
> do we all sleep on islands that fear discovery.
> [*Who Was* p.47]

> as if poured into silence. [*Who Was* p.40]

This is also, as Keats also knew, about mortality. If you try for
the immortal, if you yearn towards some Platonic ideal, you will
fail. In the Nightingale Ode, even as the bird flies off into the
infinite, the poet realises, finally, that the movement cannot be
made. Beyond death, the nightingale would still be singing, but
the poet would hear nothing, would himself be mere earth:

> Still wouldst thou sing, and I have ears in vain-
> To thy high requiem become a sod'[10]

or again, 'Sometimes existence is a threat. / To an acceptance of
death. / To gently, gently, removing want'. [*Who Was* p.46]

Poetic creativity is a question of self-annihilation or *selbst-
uberwindung*. As Nietzsche put it: 'And life confided the secret to

me: behold, it said, I am that which must always overcome itself'.[11]So:

> What do you see
> when you sleep gazing into blindness? Though
> you are round and silent
> there is a pinprick of pain you lean towards.
> The steady thud of blood
> builds up over your world –
> no one knows
> this living with annihilation. [*Who Was* p.57]

No, the poet is still here on earth, still yearning for perfection, and yet he has discovered at least something – that the movement is there to be made, not through dying, not through drink, but through poesy. Here is a book that is exemplary in both senses of the word: as an example of loss and failure and as a model of how to let the poetic be itself.

> I awake without history,
> touching strange hands.
> There are mirrors in long corridors that no
> longer give back names.
> Like a portrait
> in which the background so dominates only a
> faint cry is there
> where a fleck of whiteness was,
> I am the room without me. [*Who Was* p.81]

> He wades into the topography of night.
> The stars plot the course of his vanishing:
> man who mistook the scattered chaotic suns
> for an alphabet. [*Who Was* p.45]

David Pollard 2020

Endnotes

1 Letter 32 to George and Thomas Keats 21.12.1817 in H.E. Rollins (ed.), *The Letters of John Keats*, (Cambridge UP, 1958). Vol:1 p 53. 1:193(45).

2 *Ibid.*

3 Letter 94 to George and Thomas Keats 14 to 31.10.1818, *Ibid.* Vol 1 p.403.

4 William Hazlitt, 'Lectures on the English Poets' in P.P. Howe (ed.), *The Complete Works*, (London, Dent, 1930) vol 5, p. 47.

5 Herman Philipse, *Heidegger's philosophy of Being: a Critical Interpretation*, (Princeton UP, 199) p.205.

6 Letter 23 to George and Georgiana Keats, 14.2 to 3.5.1819 in H.E. Rollins (ed.), *The Letters of John Keats*, (CUP, 1958).Vol 2 p.80.

7 Letter 93 to Richard Woodhouse 27.10.1818, in *Ibid.* Vol 1 p.387

8 William Hazlitt, 'Lectures on the English Poets' in P.P. Howe (ed.), *The Complete Works*, (Dent, 1930) vol. 5, , p. 47.

9 Jorge Luis Borges, 'Everything and Nothing' in *Labyrinths*, (Penguin,1970) p.284.

10 John Keats, 'Ode to a Nightingale' in *John Keats*, Ed: Miriam Arlott, (Longmans Annotated English Poets, 1972) p.529.

11 Friedrich Nietzsche sec.XXXIV 'Of Self-overcoming' in *Thus Spake Zarathustra*, trans. Walter Kaufmann (Penguin, 1995) p. 295.